How Black Ops Military stopped Ascension

How Black Ops Military stopped Ascension

Transhumanism - End of the Human Era

Sam Jenkins

authorHOUSE®

AuthorHouse™
1663 Liberty Drive
Bloomington, IN 47403
www.authorhouse.com
Phone: 1-800-839-8640

Published by AuthorHouse   08/10/2015

ISBN: 978-1-4817-3207-9 (sc)
ISBN: 978-1-4817-3206-2 (e)

Library of Congress Control Number: 2013904998

Print information available on the last page.

For legal purposes only, I state that this book is a work of "fiction."
I'm a prisoner, American born and raised with ancestry that goes back well before the Revolutionary war. Yet, although I have almost no proof, I've been tortured daily over the past 15 months worse than GITMO prisoners. At least they have attorneys. At least the world knows about them.

Foreword

If you control every mind on the planet then you fully control the planet. Given that, geopolitics is mostly a red herring for the masses and a great one at that. Just theatre. Archons already loosely rule the planet and the infrastructure for full global mind control is already set up as far as I can tell; it's just a matter of flipping the switch and implementing it for everyone. This could happen in stages, as it has been on a small scale, or in one fell swoop.

There's no question that the literal "robotization" of humans is under way right now. The worst part is the heist of the human soul.

This is my story. For the most part the action starts in 2010. The story is insane, and true. It's based almost entirely on my personal experiences in this waking nightmare that started with multiversal-multidimensional communication with real aliens, incredible lucid dreams and experiences which were followed by fake alien abductions and then encounters with the sick American military.

It's about existence—not life—as a MILAB. It's about MK-Ultra with identical elements from Ritual Abuse, unfathomable evil and ignorance by a team that considers themselves military elite. It's about the spiritual war between God/Celestials and evil/Transhumansim (aka "Singularity"). It's about the death of mankind, and worse, the literal stealing of human souls by the American military on behalf of the dark side. I've tried to write this book in a reasonably chronological fashion. I will suggest the reader actually not start at Chapter One though but rather at Chapter Eight. The significance of the military industrial complex's assault on God should be the take-away content of this book.

The reader should know that I fully believe I was put on this planet to help mankind, "was" being the key word. I see humanity as a bad car wreck that I'm driving by. I'd rather not look. It's very troubled and toxic. I wouldn't touch it with a ten foot pole. I must be nothing more than a bystander who turns away.

As I say, the story is not fiction yet it's more insane and unbelievable than science fiction. I challenge you to research the technology mentioned and events that have transpired since September 11, 2001, and connect the dots. I will not martyr myself by needlessly disclosing classified information. In the end, you believe me or you don't.

I ask the reader to consider:

1. The adage: "Those who talk don't know, and those who know don't talk."
2. Anyone or anything not of this world . . . anything or anyone with supernatural or paranormal qualities that is discovered by the military industrial complex will be

seized <u>covertly</u>. If we are talking about a person that person will be electronically sequestered (imprisoned) in a type of house arrest and their home will become an invisible laboratory; as well they will be studied and picked apart and mined in every conceivable way in military/government laboratories and hospitals and they may never even be aware of it. If need be they can, of course, disappear to a government laboratory or mental hospital and then eventually be killed or have an unfortunate stroke that makes them a vegetable.

3. What kinds of technologies in medicine, cybernetics, transportation, etc., might exist in the year 2120? Given the secrecy of the military industrial complex how do you know that they don't exist now? Consider the deathbed confession of Lockheed Skunk Works CEO Ben Rich.

CHAPTER 1

It's funny how we come into this world crying, kicking and screaming.

I almost didn't make it at childbirth. My mother was a cigarette smoker who was probably sucking in a pack and a half a day when she was pregnant with me. I was born breach with complications in head and heart grasping for life.

My earliest memories are punctuated with feelings and ideas that I just didn't fit in or belong here, that my mother and father aren't my real parents, and that humans are ignorant and dangerous.

I am a civilian. I've never served in any of the armed forces.

> ➤ Definition of a MILAB: a person who is covertly abducted and impressed into covert military service by Special Operations groups within the military. They can be civilians like myself, ex-military and possibly current military personnel. This is a person with skills, abilities or special properties that makes them an asset and/or a test subject to experiment on.

I essentially died in December 2011 when a US Navy SEALs black ops group inducted me as a MILAB. I already had some super-soldier training from another black ops branch of the military, which I'll call "Branch A," a bit earlier but now I was fully converted into a 'super soldier' type entity—a transhuman. My every thought, emotion and movement was monitored and, further, totally controllable by handlers/controllers. I was soon to lose my sense of "me." I was to lose my nature, my essence and become almost totally synthetic. I have not had a real dream since probably November 2011. They are all created by my handlers. When you dream you are connected to the spiritual realm. They cannot allow this. They intercept it and then wake you, usually inserting a staged memory dream, an implanted one that plays like a movie in the mind as you wake up.

It's now February 2013. The past year has been the most bizarre and horrible year of my *existence*. As I say, my life ended when they de-humanized me. As I write this I am in an electro-magnetic force field, semi-lobotomized. The front right part of my head is tightened and pulsing, under pressure, and now the controller-torturer at the base is creating small throbbing pains in my legs and feet, having fun with me. They see every word I write. Actually they read it in my brain waves (thoughts) before my finger even hits the keyboard. This level of control is coming to you and the other seven billion plus people on this planet.

—

Mankind is dead. I'll repeat, mankind is dead. And I'm laughing.

Schematic for remote control of humans, facilitating full neurological and biological control of the target with augmented nanotechnology piggybacking on and within the human.

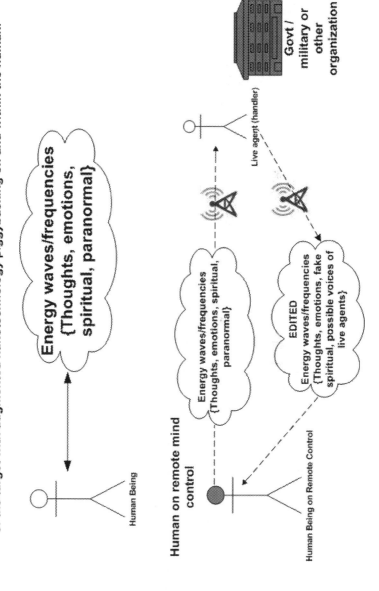

* This obviously is a simple diagram. The actual technologies and heterodyning content flow are complicated as you'd expect in a system that can accomplish a real-time or simulated real-time effect. Depending on the target and their purpose more exotic technologies may be employed.

CHAPTER 2

MILABs are Targeted Individuals

There is loud ringing and hissing in my ears, along with background talking. This is from the nano-implants the bastards put in me. Since late December 2011 the bastards (SEAL controllers) have been talking to me non-stop via synthetic telepathy. This alone would be enough to drive most people to suicide. And in fact some Targeted Individuals, especially MILABs, do commit suicide. The other common destination is a psych ward.

A team of perhaps six men with EEG headsets and/or other advanced electronic monitoring equipment see, hear, feel everything I do and read my thoughts faster than instantly. I'm not at liberty to explain how they can read my thoughts and respond to them seemingly simultaneously but I bet you can look up a few articles about how "scientists think they have found a way to create pockets of time and do some degree of time travel." Every time you see an article like this in a magazine or on a news website it means the technology was already developed at least ten years ago by the military industrial complex and it's just now being floated out to the public.

Although these people call themselves Navy SEALs, the better, functional definition is gangstalking domestic terrorists.

This kind of advanced neural-psychological remote-controlled technology was developed originally by DARPA and the NSA for Electronic Warfare (EW) purposes. It is being turned on the American people as well as the rest of the world; other governments and private parties (organized crime for example) have it.

- Military Industrial Complex = military and their cabalistic overlords.

➤ Question: What are some of the things that chemtrails, HAARP, GWEN towers, ELF waves and nanotechnologies might be used for?

➤ Question: The real wealth of Europe and America (basically most of what was Western Civilization) has been looted to the tune of trillions of "dollars," and enormous debt bubbles created. The taxpaying farm-animal slave is stuck with the debt. What has all this money been spent on by the archons who have swindled it away? Are the Ratchild's and Rockefellers interested in buying more mansions—or building a break-away New World Order civilization which culls and enslaves the masses?

So, what is a Targeted Individual? Anyone who is harassed by a team of professional thugs. In actuality this typically means electronic harassment. The individual got involved in something that angered someone with real power, usually government. However, if you think about it, military abductees (MILABs) who are recruited for "super soldier" and psychotronic warfare type projects are definitely targeted individuals because they are taken and used covertly against their will. Even if a MILAB at some point consents to and likes the project he will eventually become traumatized, broken and often suicidal.

Although I'm not suicidal I have been tortured horrifically. The worst part is I have to live with the torturers. The mind has no firewall. Once you have a team of gangstalking terrorists reading your every thought, to say nothing of beaming voices and thoughts into your head nearly every second, you have no privacy. Your mind is supposed to be your sanctuary, your last refuge. I'm jealous of those who are still free. I can only fantasize what it's like to have a free mind, to have a private thought, to go to the bathroom without some other dude watching me, to have sex without other dudes watching me, to go to sleep at night without a team of creeps telling me how they're going to rape my family members and I and make me do disgusting things with my body cavities while I sleep. By the way, the old tenet of hypnosis that you will only do what you are subconsciously morally ok with is not valid under mind control. To protect my family I will not discuss details of things that have been done to/with them by this team of cowardly torturers, but as a hint I mentioned SRA type abuse didn't I?

While I'll explain shortly, in the best chronological fashion I can, the chain of events involving the supernatural, aliens and the military impressment, I want to mention now that over that past 14 months (since December 2011) I've had no chance to privately process, let alone, heal any of the traumas/atrocities committed by the perpetrators because they read and respond literally to every thought. I have attended some Post Traumatic Stress Syndrome (PTSD) counseling but the perpetrators are of course sitting in, talking to me the whole time and cautioning me on what not to say.

Further, at the risk of the reader putting this book down at this point, I am going to say something clearly, once again, before you go: First it's necessary that you take a deep breath and imagine it is 100 years from now and we have the same types of technologies you saw in Star Trek, teleportation for example (the military does have them).

Military black ops groups are identifying Starseeds and other people with supernatural or paranormal abilities and are electromagnetically mapping and stealing their soul and spiritual properties. The victims usually have no idea except for maybe some lucid dreams involving military and/or weird settings and dreamscapes like a fake astral plane type of setting that might be conveyed to the victim as heaven. They are using these spiritual properties as gateways to communicate with the dead, to try to change history in the past and assumedly communicate with entities in the future; also to communicate (or try to) with angels, Celestial entities and other life forms in the Multiverse.

My MILAB experience under the "Branch A" group was mild compared to the SEALs. There were often lucid dreams of disasters. There was no synthetic telepathy. The events all occurred while abducted from my sleep. Make no mistake, I fully believe I usually was "pulled" and was in fact at a "Branch A" facility somewhere, not just lying in my bed tripping under hypnosis and exotic drugs. For a good reference on this abduction experience (being "pulled")—how it happens, what it's like—read Jim Sparks' book, *The Keepers*. In contrast, the SEALs MILAB program is full hardcore MK-Ultra, employing Ritual Abuse tactics. They are the cruelest, most evil humans I've ever encountered. They've destroyed my life and committed crimes against humanity and God. I should note though that they are not Satanists.

CHAPTER 3

The Dreamer, Dropout, Outsider

I possess a near perfect profile of a military abductee. I do not have a boastfully credible demeanor, nor have a silver tongue. Many politicians and attorneys are believable professional liars in contrast. I'm eccentric. You've heard the expression of thinking outside of the box; well I don't even see the box. I'm so right-brained it's not even funny. While I'm not a hermit and do enjoy a social life, I don't have a large social network. People like me are good candidates for experimentation and torture with things like voice-to-skull etc. This is why celebrities and high-profile people rarely are targeted for electronic harassment. Covert electronic mind control, yes; harassment, no. In short, I'm not "in band," I'm not rich and I don't have hundreds of friends and high visibility in the community.

Thank God I wasn't medicated for Attention Deficit Disorder as a kid. I spent a lot of time in class in my school years staring out the window daydreaming. I loved to read more than anything. I was reading at advanced levels at an early age and always had the highest marks in English. I loved the books on the great explorers—Magellan, Columbus, DeSoto etc.—and have always been a major history buff. My family moved a lot so I was often the new kid, and I firmly believe this contributed greatly to my sense of being an outsider. Experiencing the xenophobia (ignorance) of the stereotypes associated with being a Southerner (if we moved to the North) and visa-versa if we moved to the South resulted in me seeing what would be called mainstream sheeple as just that—easily dividable, myopic, dim and hard to respect.

Society (especially today) is a total cluster-fuck and the family structure is disintegrating. This is totally by design. The significance of having some kind of trauma in your life, especially childhood, is that it makes you a much better target for MK-Ultra; because you have already been fractured it's easier to create the alter personalities in you. Further this kind of person will have developed unique survival/coping skills. They can generally handle wild situations and trauma better than others.

I always had a major independence streak and never have hung around too long in formal groups or clubs. You can probably guess I had a little problem with authority. Many of my biggest mistakes have been from times where I tried to be "in band" too much and did what I was told, following the rules. Likewise, my biggest successes have always come from breaking the rules, dropping out and going my own direction. I am definitely not a follower. However, being *separate* was to eventually land me in the nightmare I'm in now. I cannot stress enough to Starseeds, adepts and metaphysicians, the importance of blending in, of remaining occulted in the times we are in now, for you are prime resources for harvesting by the powers that be. Trust me, you have something they want very much, something they will steal from you.

Since I was about ten I've been deeply spiritual, feeling the ineffable profoundly and often. I was into Shamanism (without having called it that) my whole life. There is a correspondent subject of interest dating back to early childhood which is actually innate in origin. It is manifested as an awareness and worldview which is very politically incorrect and ancient; it relates to an ancient and ongoing struggle in mankind—but it's best to leave this out! If I haven't alluded to this already I'll state it now: I have no interest in martyring myself for anyone. Further, I'm frazzled, disassociated and decimated on levels I didn't know even existed thanks to the hellish MK-Ultra tortures and soul-hijacking programs of the perpetrators. I have no more God-given resources with which to utilize. I can't say strongly enough, Starseeds are like prime majestic real estate which are strip-mined and left barren if the military industrial complex gets hold of them.

In the early-mid 1990's I had a prophetic dream about an event in the Northeast which I believe was the 911 attacks. This was a lucid dream. It was a lot like the movie Christmas Story: I was sort of a viewer being escorted to the setting and witnessing things.

The same thing happened in 2003. I had a lucid dream about a massive hurricane hitting the Mississippi coast (Katrina in 2005).

I developed a passion for metaphysics, you might say "applied metaphysics" during 2006. During this year I had a couple extremely interesting experiences involving what I can only call divine intervention—my life was saved in a very eerie event. I should add that I've had help from Angels at other times in my life.

During 2006 and onward I began to have contact with inter-dimensional beings, both good, bad and downright strange. In 2007 I experienced an amazing miracle that had some high strangeness, with profound synchronicities—and I believe cosmic extraterrestrial intervention. It's interesting, the significance of full moons.

I had some intense fantastical, lucid dreams in 2008 and then starting in November 2009 they started happening often. I have to leave open the possibility that some or all of these, in late 2009, were induced by the "Branch A" group. I tend to believe they were natural though because they were similar to those I had in 2008 which was prior to any military and fake alien abductions. These dreams were quite possibly connected with my interdimensional and ET friends as well as a shift in timeline energies (Ascension).

I will note that a number of people in the timeframe of 2010-2011 had powerful, lucid dreams of disasters and apocalyptic scenes. I did as well but I very strongly suspect that these were generated by the military, as I was an abductee at that time.

CHAPTER 4

Abductions

Abductions by greys, reptilians and "Nordics" are usually fake in my opinion. You are really being abducted by the military. They can easily fake the alien characters and dreamscapes with holographic screen memories. Nonetheless, the military may indeed be in contact with negative ET's and I'm by no means saying that greys and reptilians don't exist. Nordics by the way are usually benevolent. In the fake abduction experience other types of fake ET's can appear benevolent as well including greys and sometimes reptilians.

All possibilities are open as to what alien life forms the military has captured or otherwise been involved with. It is beyond my comprehension that any benevolent ET race would associate with the military at all. I have had abductions that involved tall greys, reptilians and Nordics. I believe these to be totally fake. Of course, some of the screen memories involve military personnel and doctors. Some of these abductions can be very well produced, very slick. The abductee can be left with a feeling anywhere between elation and terror. Not all encounters with aliens, whether real or fake, involve abductions. I've experienced various forms of greys and what I call little "ebens" internally in my body and consciousness. I believe both of these to have been real. The greys could have been fake but it is unlikely considering the context which made them "visible" and another factor that I cannot disclose. These varieties invade the energy body and physical body, inhabiting you that way.

Obviously I've had real contact with aliens, including fully-conscious contact. Further, anyone who tells you that the astral plane is not real and that there aren't malevolent entities there has never experienced it.

I must say, I've had paranormal walk-in types of encounters. These have happened during sleep and when awake. I also have seen what some might call Men in Black (MIB) characters. These characters were in a human-reptilian form. This has occurred in full waking conscious reality. These characters have always been in the form of black males usually in biker outfits. This may sound strange, however, in talking with James Bartley (an expert on reptilians in my opinion) this is indeed a reptilian theme and motif. These were not humans, they were not from this planet. They were reptilians and nothing I want to be involved with.

I have to ask though, aren't humans a reptilian-mammal hybrid? We know that the human fetus develops a reptilian tail early on. At one time I was really into the theories of mankind's origin, some of which include a reptilian master race which engineered us. Everyone is familiar with Enki and Enlil, the Annunaki, Draco reptilians, Lyra etc. Many of these corresponding theories are mixed with myth (which may be fact-based for all we know) but where we came from and the scattered story line(s) to it all remain hopeless mysteries—to us.

Walk-in experiences, true psi and remote communications e.g. remote viewing/sensing using pure organic mind, devic body and psychotronic crystals is another topic in itself. I am completely drained and devastated by over a year of daily electronic torture. What little, if any psi ability or properties I have left I try to sabotage so that the SEAL torturer-thieves can't use it. This was never really something I was good at directing anyway. I don't have any more remote-viewing capabilities than anybody else.

> Advice: If you experience other forms of abduction/contact (or high strangeness, supernatural events) especially ones that are positive—keep it to yourself or close friends or family. Never, I repeat NEVER post it on a website. Unfortunately, the military can simulate positive abduction experiences now and may do this to you, but they won't remain positive. You get the point; they are interested in real phenomena. They will study you like a lab rat and rip off as much as they can and on top of that they'll check out all your family members.

The military has researched and tested everyone in my family, especially my immediate family. As far as psychic qualities they're all duds, totally normal, as I already knew. I've never felt any kind of cosmic or spiritual connection to my family. Nor is there any royalty or prominence in my blood-line.

I hate the black ops military groups beyond words. They're diabolical. They're thieves of the most sacred things in life, in our Universe and Megaverse. They are not just playing God; they are assaulting and plundering God. There's a song by the band "Therapy?" called *Turn*. It's dark to be sure (kick-ass music though). The lyrics go "storming Heaven without God . . . barging into the presence of God." I've declared this the theme song of the black ops groups.

The first fake alien abduction I experienced was in March of 2010. I awoke to a lucid dream but it was different than any other dream I'd ever had. It seemed so physically real, more like the event actually happened and I was just returned to my bed. Here's how it went. I was in a medical exam room sitting on an exam table. There was a nurse that looked like she was straight out of the 1950's wearing an old style nurse's uniform. Something about her looked really plastic and fake though. I noticed at some point that her face was becoming cartoonish—like it was animated almost. Her mouth widened in an exaggerated Grinch-like smile. There was a blonde-haired male doctor sitting on a couch and he was talking casually to me. I don't remember more than that.

I knew something had actually happened and for the next week or so I couldn't get this out of my mind. Rather than recount every single abduction, I'll again refer the reader to *The Keepers*. There are many other books and websites detailing these abductions. Needless to say the abductions continued. It wasn't long after the first abduction that I experienced the first Black Helicopter episode. I was at a cabin in the mountains surrounded by tranquility. It was about 10 a.m. and suddenly I heard the loud in-your-face sound of a helicopter. It flew slowly and low right over my cabin, just above the trees, followed by two more helicopters, single file.

At some point I began noticing men in black robes and military uniforms in the abductions. This is when it got scary. One of the scenes was funny though but I cannot publicly describe it. It became clear I was involved in a black ops project and I was unnerved about it. This was against my will.

After about six months of abductions though I had apparently fallen into bad standing with this group. As a consequence

I began experiencing negative reptilian-type abductions/ dreamscapes. These are typically in settings that approximate the common depiction of Hell with excrement everywhere, and forms of heartbreak and tragedy. I don't wish to expound on this. Some of James Bartley's writings are a good source if you wish to explore this. I cannot elaborate on these events or this subject further. The punishments pale in comparison to what the SEALs team did/does to me though. Further, I believe that should I have ceased the activities that offended them they may have left me alone. Nor did the "Branch A" group ever use synthetic telepathy (putting voices and thoughts in my head).

I could go on at length about details of MILAB/super-soldier experiences. Ditto for other topics that would put my life at even greater risk than it already is. Trust me, you want God, not man-made, synthetic experiences.

I will say, on the bright side, that the medical treatment I received from all the black ops groups has been top quality and far advanced beyond what is available to civilians. As one of my handlers put it: what the public has isn't healthcare, it's wildlife management.

Under the "Branch A" group I remember having heart surgery. It took two nights to perform. The memory I have is of aliens doing it and it was a strange procedure. I'd guess it was just a screen memory, and whatever was done was by human doctors. I've had other treatments for various health problems as well. It doesn't mean that they like me. In the military's view I'm a piece of equipment they own and therefore maintain. That's all.

CHAPTER 5

MILAB to the Max

Around October 2011 the nature of the military abductions began to change. I began to see small aircraft fly over my house on nights when abductions would take place. Often these would start around dusk, and often if I stepped outside on the front porch just before going to bed a plane would be coming right towards me. Almost without fail, on full moons I'd get abducted and there would be a memory of myself with a team of other guys. Some of the settings were of a bonding nature with fraternal type activities which I would describe as a bit dark and immoral.

In November I had a very powerful and unusual abduction which again I must generalize as follows. It was Thanksgiving night and I was staying at my mother's house on a small farm nearby. This abduction involved an alien that was a good guy but for certain concerns which I'll respect I won't mention the type. I'd had a few of these before. This particular one involved a rescue type mission as had one of the previous ones. At the time, I actually believed this form of alien was real. Actually, to the best of my knowledge there are real versions of them and several previous experiences bear this out.

There was a unique twist to this abduction though at the end which seemed very odd. Also I was told at the end of it, "keep your mouth shut."

The next morning however military aircraft was CONSTANTLY overhead. Literally everywhere I went, day and night, non-stop and it didn't begin to taper off until late spring of 2012. People talk about the "black helicopter" experience. You can't even imagine. I had constant large chemtrails over my house and neighborhood, wherever I worked, wherever I went. There were long white, slow-flying aircraft over my house and alongside the street whenever I'd go for walks, all the time. These would usually be the first craft I would see when walking out into my driveway every morning, one after another. At times I had endless processions of military planes flying single-file over my house at night. I'd stand out front and watch in bewilderment.

The perpetrators began abducting me nearly every night, and also started to roll in the synthetic telepathy. Things were changing fast. I didn't know it but I was being impressed into this group big time. It was pure harassment though and scary. I was being awoken numerous times at night typically between 1 and 6 a.m., and left with screen memories, always intimidating and harsh but often intriguing, sometimes nightmarish and cruel. Occasionally they were good. The point is to traumatize you and break you down. They totally invade your life and this is the beginning process of it. You get no chance to stop and think or rest. They psychologically break you down. It's the equivalent of boot camp. As a man it's easy to romanticize military stuff like this in retrospect. Who wouldn't want to be inducted into a supposedly elite military group? So I describe it accurately, it's MK-Ultra that uses the same components of Ritual Abuse. That's exactly what they did. Yes there were good times, funny times and sometimes they helped me with some things but mostly it was hell and has become a living hell. Such is the path of the MILAB. Living with synthetic telepathy and inside of a frequency fence (force field), it's a destination of suicide or a mental hospital. You just try to live as long as you can.

I tried to explain what was happening to my younger brother and other family and predictably they said I needed to be on medicine. Typical response for all Targeted Individuals, especially MILABs with experiences like mine. Like most other normal people he's only capable of tenured thought. Any idea or story that falls outside of his narrow belief system is dismissed and replaced with "mental illness" or other pre-supplied responses. He thought the countless military planes flying low over my house one evening were airliners, theorizing they were descending to the airport south of us. He didn't have much response when I placed a compass on the table; the planes were flying north. The perpetrators taunted me with the situation. They knew I really had nowhere to turn to. After trying to explain more to my brother one morning I walked outside only to be greeted by a low-flying Blackhawk type helicopter right over my driveway. They of course knew he was inside and wouldn't see it.

I figured I was being hit by microwave beams causing the voice-to-skull (synthetic telepathy) and tried to shield myself. I had an electrician build me a faraday cage. It did not work. I tried all kinds of magnets and tin-foil hat type stuff. Nothing works except a military-grade frequency jammer which is prohibitively expensive and hard to get as a civilian.

In early 2012 I was taken for a spin by other branches of the military and possibly some intelligence agencies. I believe the Air Force or Air Command was one, as well as some unit of the

"Branch A" group again. I did have some exciting times. I was a very, very big ticket item. Top generals were interested in me. I saw and experienced some things that were, you might say, beyond this world! I was actually promised various rewards which is unheard of.

I'll never forget this night. I was sleeping on the floor underneath a crude covering of mylar blankets and I got abducted numerous times. Even if I understood the scientific details behind fractal jumpgate technology I would not discuss it since it's so protected. Trust me, you can be "taken" multiple times and for prolonged periods without missing any linear time.

On this occasion I was taken to what I assumed was the Moon but cannot confirm. No, there wasn't a big sign that said "Welcome to the Moon" but I clearly had the impression it was off world. I was inside a huge facility with craft and machinery. It was very other-worldly. There were reptilians as well. They were clustered around the walls of the facility. How much of this setting was real and how much was purely a staged holographic memory I'm not sure. I was told, "You asked about compensation?" then shown a huge house and was told this would be for my family.

I forgot to mention that upon waking up in my bed or on the floor after many of these abductions I'd be panting and in a pumped up state. See, it was all a sleep disorder!

On another night I was in a research facility being shown around. There were offices which displayed covert inventions. I was told by personnel that "great things always share one another." I was shown a room at one point with spying equipment in it. There were perhaps five or six people, one of whom was a woman with short hair who was explaining something to me about surveillance. Later I found myself sitting down in a room and in walked my best friend from college. We got into a fight but it was all in good-nature, more like sparing. I had been sleeping on my living room floor that night with a loaded AK and various gadgets I thought I might be able to use to repel the abductors. At this time I was still resisting. When I awoke I was again panting as if on some kind of good adrenaline-like drug and despite the usual shock of it I felt good. I told another MILAB friend who I'd discovered, about it the next day, explaining that things were getting better.

Also, there were other types of mission abductions, sometimes with a good reward. One was what I believe may have been a type of initiation involving an execution. Most likely this was a holographic dream though. I also don't remember actually killing anybody.

What I've just described were basically the glory days and that's as good as it got. The rest is pure hell. I can tell you honestly that every MILAB I know of is miserable and abused. At their best they lie to themselves. I did and still do; you have to be delusional in order to survive this mentally. That's what PTSD is all about.

Perhaps many years from now I'll write about this chapter of my life in more detail. For now I have to say somberly that this is all dark and scary. I wish it never happened. Further, I was "flash in the pan." They made me out to be more than I was, and they ended up hating me.

I did my best to resist early on. Unfortunately, I made every mistake by trying to fight. That's what they like and want. I will offer some tips on how to get out of this later.

PTSD and Stockholm Syndrome

As the months went by and I learned more about what was going on it dawned on me that I was in a kind of mafia. I got nervous because of the secrecy I had to maintain, and on top of that I've had tortures usually every single night, most of which are—EVIL.

Because of this, my personal life being fully read and known in great detail and exploited by the perpetrators and the general unreality of this ordeal, I developed PTSD.

I tried to tell them early on that I was not fit for this and I simply can't handle synthetic telepathy. It makes me crazy—I cannot control my thoughts—and it's by your thoughts and inner voice that you communicate back to the controllers. Imagine your common inner dialog but instead of self talk you direct it to a remote party. After a while, unfortunately you learn to do this. It requires creating new neural pathways. I wish I could erase these, unlearn this. The handlers taught me how to do this and it's baked into me now, regrettably. What you basically do is push the inner voice downward and back rather than projecting outward as you would to someone in person. I'd love to be able to unlearn this so I could at least be mute.

The mind has no firewall

When every single thought you have is instantly read and a near-simultaneous response from a controller follows it—it's game over. If someone else knows your every thought there's nothing you can think or do to defeat them, to get away from them. You're screwed. Worse, you effectively lose your *life*. You also, under constant thought communication, become conditioned to patterns of responses—waiting for responses from them etc. The innermost parts of you cease to exist. I remember deep sorrow in April 2012, even on days when things were relatively ok. I'd be crying inside and I wasn't sure why but I am now. It was for the loss of myself.

I started "saying" vicious, vulgar things to them automatically. Ask yourself, where do thoughts come from? Whether it's your subconscious, aspects of your deepest self (unconscious depths) or wherever one thing is for sure, 'you' don't manufacture a thought. The mind typically incessantly chatters anyway. Again, involuntarily I began calling them pretty nasty names and making very gross mentally verbal statements about them, their families and kids etc. Why? Because of the tortures they did to me, especially involving my family. Remember, ritual abuse (SRA) was/is used by them against me and this involves unmentionable atrocities involving family members. The more I had these involuntary retaliatory thoughts the more they beat on me via electronic torture and lucid nightmares. Amazingly the controllers believed I had control of my thoughts. I think they finally realize this is impossible now. Unlike them, when they communicate to me, I don't get to edit my thoughts. I have no privacy. How can you not have negative, vengeful thoughts about someone who kept you up all night torturing you?

MILABs are also under constant watch, every single second. The military knows the high suicide risk for these assets. It has pumped many millions of dollars into the MILAB and must protect it to the fullest; ironically, at least in the SEALs group, they beat the living hell out of you. I can't discuss this much more except to say that in my case it is prolonged and extreme.

While there are support groups for typical Targeted Individuals, like Freedom From Covert Harassment and Surveillance (FFCHS), there are none for MILABs.

I found myself stuck between the perpetrators and a society that was in some ways even worse than them. You cannot go to the police, FBI or CIA for help. Good luck with even family and friends. In fact, it cost me my relationship with part of my family. This is common for Targeted Individuals. God help you if you end up in court trying to keep your kids and explaining your situation to a judge. Fortunately, I quickly realized that I had to play and use everyone as best I could and lie my ass off if necessary. You must lie. You must play the best cards you can.

If you seek a counselor you have to be extremely careful about who you choose and screen them first or you risk being put in a mental hospital. I've put a tip for this at the end of this chapter for MILABs.

As awful and sick as it is, I found myself bonding with my captors, my torturers, because they are the only ones who fully believe me. It's tantamount to someone being put in a cell with a rapist and whenever they're released they're quickly thrown back in for reporting it to a disbelieving public. Who's worse? Also, like them, I am outside the mainstream. In that sense I related much more to them than to the sheeple, despite the MK-Ultra tactics.

Combine this with the military conditioning and other aspects of a fraternity where loyalty, unity and defense and a common cause are instilled into you and you get a major case of Stockholm Syndrome. I looked up the treatment for Stockholm Syndrome. The first step is to get away from the perpetrators. But I can't do that. I'm stuck with them until I die or a miracle occurs. Making this much worse is the fact that they control my brain function. Some call this neural-psychology. They can control your mood, disposition, self-image, enact different alter personalities, and of course torture you mentally in myriad ways that defy description . . . all remotely. They can make you feel like a clown, like a Gomer Pyle, which is one of the alters they used when breaking me down in the initial break-in phase. I'm always in a force field, and sometimes in "total lockdown." The brief times they let me out to be myself, I'm still under control but it just doesn't feel like it as much. At any rate, when they have me strongly under control (they call this "having their finger on me") the Stockholm Syndrome can really kick in on ridiculous levels.

I hope the reader can see that I'm totally subjugated and that it's all deniable! I sound like a paranoid schizophrenic. Electronic mind control and torture though is being inflicted on many thousands of people right here in America by the government and military. It is also being used by other governments, organized crime and other private parties who have obtained it through ex-military, crooked defense contractors or other channels.

Listen to me! I'm a piece of equipment, remote controlled by a dark faction of the military. Literally. My head is a cell-phone with full duplex communication. That's all I am. The technology really isn't that remarkable. I'll say again, it's wrong, it's evil. This alone is the nail in the coffin of mankind.

➢ Homework assignments:

1. Watch the Jesse Ventura documentary on Targeted Individuals, *Brain Invaders*.
2. Look up "Singularity"—the concept of when humans and computers merge (reference Ray Kurzweil). Do

    a Google search on the up-coming next generation of computers that aren't controlled by mice and keyboards but by your brain waves.

3. Look at commercially available EEG sensors and headgear by NeuralSky and others for interfacing micro-electronic games and other devices. Look up "synthetic telepathy aka artificial telepathy".

4. Read about the new "Brain Mapping" project.

➢ Question: Where does all this technology originate? If rinky-dink versions of it are only now trickling into the consumer markets for stupid gizmos how advanced do you think hidden applications of it are?

➢ Question: If you wanted to rule the world wouldn't it be stupid to bomb it to smithereens in old-fashioned styled wars?

Instead of being a multi-million dollar asset I'm now a broken down, self-sabotaging, self-defeating loser. Like the Springsteen song says, "end up like a dog that's been beat too much." And frankly I'd rather be down and out than be an asset to the monsters.

A logical question many people have for the MILAB is how can you be in your bed at home and simultaneously at a military base or hospital? The term for this was mentioned earlier in this book. It's something you saw in star-trek.

➢ In the early days of my induction into the SEALs I reluctantly told a family member what was happening—I more-less spilled my guts about the basics. The response from the handlers was the carrot and stick that night. I'll pass on describing the carrot. The stick was that I woke up the next morning with significant bruises all over my biceps. I've been threatened with more of this, for example, waking up with large patches of my head shaved or with black eyes or an eyelid sliced and pulled down over my eye. One thing they threatened a lot was my pet's tail cut off and lying beside me and future, more severe warnings of his head cut off. They haven't done these things yet but can. They say, how would you like to go to the doctor after waking up with facial injuries—what would you tell him? Tell him the truth and you go to a psych ward on top of that. They're correct.

Am I mad about all this? How do I feel about the retarded tv-owning cockroach slave who provides the police force, "mental health" community—infrastructure—for this torture prison planet for the sentient? I can answer that with the below question.

How does it feel American or European idiot tax slave? . . .

Your country and civilization are GONE, its wealth totally looted and replaced with incalculable debt bubbles. The bankster-archons essentially have a magic credit card with no limit and you and your offspring pay the bill eternally. Where did/does the real wealth (money energy) go? Where is it? Do the Ratchilds, Windsors and Bilderberger bunch spend it on new yachts—maybe they need a new Rolls Royce or Lear jet?

Here stupid, they spend it on a separate break-away civilization with space-age technologies which among other things already can increase longevity possibly indefinitely (overcoming death)—a disparate hegemonic civilization which you will simply be a *total* slave to. To all the two-legged farm animals who call me mentally ill, who drive around in crude carts made of metal-fiberglass, four rubber tires and an antique combustible engine from the industrial revolution, who live shitty pain-filled "lives" until maybe a whopping 75 and think they have it made, while I pay an exorbitant price for merely knowing great truths, a part of me relishes watching your pathetic scurrying meaningless ignorance-addicted rat-asses go down the drain.

Now for my good side:

> Tip for a MILAB in selecting a counselor:

If you can't find others to talk to in person or you need a counselor to vouch for you for whatever reason, here is a warning and a tip. The belief system of the average person and mental health "professional" doesn't support ideas outside of tenured thought. They're robots. There's a good chance, if you trust a robot, you'll be on your way to medication and/or a mental hospital.

1) Try to find a counselor who is familiar with MK-Ultra, Monarch programming, alter personalities, and if possible psi-ops and shadow government awareness. Always interview them on the phone before even visiting. A good choice can be someone who advertises themselves as a "Christian" counselor. Why? Because they already get the concept of "Satanic Cults" and will probably be familiar with "satanic ritual abuse." SRA is identical to MILAB (MK-Ultra programming). From that angle they will likely believe you. Always tell them from the beginning that if they say one thing about schizophrenia or medication you are going to get up and leave.

2) In general when you explain something that's hard to believe to a skeptic, never overdo it with swearing that it's true and they

must believe you. Don't try to ram it down them, try to talk calmly. If they don't believe something you say just move on. If the situation deteriorates then leave.

TIPS for anyone who suddenly wakes up one morning and hears voices in their head

Welcome to hell. You are now a Targeted Individual. You may well be for life. This is the most critical time to take action. Do not wait!

Do not be passive. Don't try to deny that it's happening. If you are in bed, don't just lay there and think "oh that's strange." (That's what I did at first). Instead flip out. ANYTIME YOU HEAR A VOICE IN YOUR HEAD YOU HAVE A MAJOR PROBLEM. Treat it just like you would a heart attack. The rest of the world stops! Do not go into work, do not try to carry on as usual. These voices are real humans and they do not have your best interest in mind.

Your thoughts—every one of them—are being read by one or more "gangstalkers." They may be military, a Gestapo branch of the government like "homeland security" or organized crime.

Go crazy! Run around screaming. *EXTREME CAUTION HERE (for legal reasons of the author): Threaten to kill yourself. Take out a knife or unloaded gun and just keep it close by but DO NOT actually try to harm yourself or others.

Say to yourself, "if they can talk to me then they can read my thoughts too. They are in my brain. They can see what I see, hear what I hear . . ." Then proceed to do everything imaginable to gross them out. Pull out all the stops.

The great odds are that your perpetrators are straight males. Get on the Internet and look at tons of gay porn. You'll get desensitized to it after a while. They won't. It's good to go for the interracial variety so that whatever race(s) they may be you'll get to them. You may want to print out some of the pictures and place them around your house so you inadvertently see them just walking around. This packs a nastier punch. When you premeditate something harmful to them they can filter it, otherwise they can't. Obviously, if you have a family you can't use this tactic.

Pull up every gross or otherwise negative memory you can! Keep doing it nonstop. Dwell graphically on the time that . . . this or that . . . happened. Take your time when in the bathroom and focus more on things you normally wouldn't. Maybe you want to focus more on that after you leave. Visualize unpleasant body parts in personal sensory detail. You get the idea.

There's a caveat to the above tactics. The perpetrators can do the same things to you but immeasurably worse. However, if you react like this from the beginning the odds are they won't. They may leave. If you are already a Targeted Individual and you try this you may only have limited success but it's worth a try.

Do not call the police. Do not call relatives. Do not call a psychologist. You are asking for major trouble if you do and will be playing into the perpetrator's hands. They want to drive you insane. They want to make you destroy yourself.

Do not let someone else tell you or even suggest to you that you might have a mental issue. Don't waste your time trying to convince anybody who can't even grasp that this is reality.

CHAPTER 6

Lab Rat to the Max

The title of this chapter says it all. The SEALs black ops group liked me not for my physical abilities. Yes I was into survivalist stuff and had an interest in fighting but I'm a forty-something and over the hill. We may have shared some common views on some things as well, but my soul is not for rent or sale.

I can say that although I am a Starseed I am not a total "Love and Light" kind. On some levels I am but honestly I have quite a mean streak, although I'd prefer to call it a "survival streak."

Why am I still in this program? What are they using me for? The answer to this is why I'm writing this book. This is the bizarre and sick thing that I must publish. My former main controller told me a while back I was in the "psychic warrior" program. More honest handlers however told me that what I am is glorified lab rat. That's correct.

They use me:

- As a stargate to communicate with other intelligences in the Multiverse.
- To communicate with the dead.

- And for other things that I cannot talk about and yet more I don't even want to know about.

How do they do this? They use my SOUL. They can open up my chakras and induce deep soul/psycho-spiritual communication waves. Yep, just like you have an aura which is an energy field. The soul and spiritual essence have unique frequency signatures. They capture and map these and beam these into space as well as use them for certain purposes. They try to get these auric properties to talk to Angels and other Celestial beings, among other things.

This horrifies and pisses me off beyond words. Upon fully grasping this is when I decided to resume total resistance and go public.

I should clarify something. The incredible multidimensional multiversal Ascension *trips* I used to have, have been totally monitored, captured, studied and used by the invader thieves since December 2011. The term the handlers dubbed these with was "schisms." I describe these later. They used me, as I said, when they had me at "their place" as they call it. I know where the facility is where they keep my clone. It's a very prominent medical research facility here in the city I live in, in the Southeast. I believe the military base the handlers operate out of is a large local Air Force Base about 20 miles from my house and possibly another one in a state to my west. However, the medical and way-out experiments and psychic projects are almost surely done at the medical facility. I'm almost positive of that.

It's March 2013. As the awesome Ascension trips tapered off almost completely over the past few months some of the cruelest handlers, the ones who hate me the most, told me at times that I'd be "put back" to how I was but without any psychic abilities.

Why? So I won't be a threat to them or to mankind, they say. This is indeed what they've done. I don't know how it all works, only that they've somehow mapped these energies/powers to my clone (they tell me this too), bypassing me. Supposedly I am much more synthetic now. It feels like it. My clone is probably closer to the real me. As I understand it they have swapped body parts with my clone. Also I've been told that I'm kind of a chop suey of body parts. I've found out from other MILABs that the swapping of body parts for psychic related reasons is indeed done. As I type this they're telling me how I'm crossing a line . . . they're going to really punish me and besides that nobody will believe this anyway. So be it.

Can you imagine how I feel? Has anybody ever been robbed like this?

But there are two things dear reader that make me feel better. Something Light Beings (discussed in the next chapter) shared with me on a visit in fall of 2011; and the fact that mankind is dead—already dead. I know that sounds strange but I promise the Mayans had it right. The invaders did not fully rip me off in time. Read on.

The black ops handlers frequently send me mocked extrasensory Ascension trips that they ripped off from me! That's right, my own stuff. They can mock it very well. It feels good but it's fake. It's not coming from another dimension; it's coming from some asshole at a computer. They'll broadcast this into me, saying "here, does this cheer you up?"

This brings up another point. Why are they letting me write this book? There are reasons.

Think about it. Lots of insiders write books; sometimes they pay a horrible price.

I haven't described the religion they are but it's all bullshit to me. Evil is evil. What they are doing is assaulting God and the Heavens. They're constructing synthetic dimensions and who knows what else based on rip-offs of Celestial energies. One thing they can easily do is fake a "second coming" of Jesus etc., by taking ineffable experiences they've captured from Starseeds and then beaming these into groups of people, as I've just described. They can also put the "voice of God" into their head via synthetic telepathy. This could easily be done to, let's say, the entire Christian population of the USA.

It makes me want to vomit knowing that these bastards are surely already using *my* sacred energies/properties on various people they want to "turn on" to let them think they're spiritual or special. This is common for new MILABs—along with the hazing they'll tell you that you have unusual powers to pump you up, and also to make you think you are part of a special team. They may tell a new recruit or MILAB that they all have this ability too; "we're a small group with special abilities, we're all like this."

They studied the living hell out of me. There have been periods of time when another group was brought in to study me (I think the regular Navy or Navy Intelligence) and they induced these neural-chakra openings throughout the day to open psychic channels. They did this nearly every day in October 2012 while I was at work. A handler with a different personality would talk to me like a twisted "doctor" talking to a subdued lab rat. There may have been scientists and doctors on hand or otherwise tied in real-time during these experiments. These neural-chakra openings, in plain English, make you horny. The target will feel sexual energy boiling up.

Another thing is whenever you have sex they capture the psychic energy in and around you. They are looking for interdimensional entities that may be present and also using the energy for various other purposes. No further comment.

Also, I should say that I supposedly have a child, a baby son, via this group. I may have many more for all I know. To my knowledge other MILAB groups do this as well. The reader may wish to explore this topic in *The Keepers* as well as search and read about it online. I'll be clear. They would never allow me in waking life to see this child, nor probably even in "their place" as they call it. Actually, because I've been excommunicated and I fully disavow them and reject the child, they have put him up for adoption.

Of all the lowest, most shameful events this group has done to me, this one has to rank among the worst. On the anniversary of my brother's death a handler told me to leave work early and go home and grieve. It wasn't hard for him to induce me to do this. Remember, they have full control of your limbic system, of your entire brain and emotional structure via a neural programming API in the implant.

So I was crying while sitting at my kitchen table and looking out of the window, when I heard a "spotter" voice saying to the handler back at the base . . . "that's it, I think he's getting some communication, I think we have something . . ."

I heard it as clear as day. There was brief silence then the "spotter" said "he heard me . . . we're busted," or words to that effect.

I just sat there in stony silence thinking "that's it—they have to leave me alone now."

They laid off a little but were back full force in a couple days.

As I said they are interested in capturing communications with the dead. Look at it this way. Imagine recording a phone call or a conversation in a room. You are recording frequency waves—energy waves. It's the same thing.

Near Death Experience (NDE) Experiments

One of the sickest, scariest things they've done to me is use me in NDE experiments. I'm not at liberty to discuss this more due to vociferous threats. Connect the dots yourself if you can; what is an age-old type of travel scientists have been interested in and worked on? I'll never forget the time in spring 2012 when I came home from work, laid down for a nap on my bed and when I woke up I was totally disoriented like I've never experienced before. It was about what you'd think it would be like coming back from "the other side." I can recall a couple other occasions where they did this. The environment for this was the same. There was a white background where I was taking huge leaps across space and time it seemed. It was very creepy. I was extremely angry when I came out of this. The idea that I would consent to this is outrageous. They later started referring to this exercise as the "bunny hop."

> ➤ A common affirmation I do is: "I will everything the military uses me for to backfire <u>on them</u> catastrophically."

I know that they have done NDE experiments much more often when I'm at their base or hospital. Also, I know they use two of my family members (one being my elderly mother) to *assist* me sometimes when I'm at the base/lab in these kinds of operations. This is how sick they are. The use of supporting family members or friends is common knowledge among others like me in these experiments. Much thanks to the very brave people who have discussed this with me. By the way, my mother underwent similar "enhancement" surgery to me around the same time my induction into the SEALs started.

Yes, it's all real, all too real. They abduct and operate on you and you can do what about it?

They've researched and tested everyone in my family, especially my immediate family. As far as psychic qualities they're all duds, as I already knew. I've never felt any kind of cosmic or spiritual connection to my family. They're all normal.

I've also been able to piece together from staged memories in the early days that I'm often in a kind of hospital/dorm setting when at "their place." I can't describe the hatred I have for these mad monsters.

Controlled Deaths

Another thing they will likely do when/if they kill me is to map where "I" go to after death, "I" meaning my soul. Alternatively they may try to keep my soul in some kind of synthetic environment—less likely though. Given the former, what they will do is have family members (under covert abduction) try to communicate with me "on the other side" from their laboratory.

They will do this to study the "other side" more and to manipulate it, to learn how to have departed souls perform miracles for them.

In the future this level of control is coming to all surviving humans. They will decide who gets to reincarnate. They'll possibly direct souls to some kind of synthetic dimension. As a visual, I go with the scene from *The Matrix* of the babies in the dark laboratory setting with all the tubes and wiring coming out of them. They were in a stasis and their souls used as batteries if I remember correctly.

I know already they've done extensive experiments having me communicate with guardian angels as well as dead relatives as I've said before.

The Celestials, my star family, that brought me into this world is not in favor of these pigs, to put it gently. Angels, Heaven, Divine Benevolence is forever barred from them, and will forever keep them here in this plastic, damned world. More on that later.

CHAPTER 7

Light Beings and Other ET's

What a Light Being isn't: Some dude who channels Archangel Michael or someone or something related to an "Ashtar" in the "Galactic Federation."

A Light Being is a very, very, very cool Extra-terrestrial. Yes, a REAL one.

I've had a number of encounters with them, each time incredible and love-filled. They can communicate verbally but internally. They actually enter you and possess you. They are like a best friend in a way. They can heal you—especially mentally and emotionally. Most of all they hate the black ops military. As words can't describe my hate for the black ops groups, neither can they describe my love for my star family.

I've had encounters with them in waking consciousness. I know of a couple other people who have as well and describe similar experiences. However, it is indeed only a very few people I'm aware of who've had this contact. I urge in the strongest terms for those who have to be quiet about it.

There are a number of people who experience "light orbs" a.k.a "balls of light." I'm quite convinced, connecting some dots, these are the exact same things.

I consider myself closer to Light Beings than I do humans, to put it mildly. The best feeling I can have towards man is a kind of pity. Some Starseed I am!

The only other thing I wish to share about Light Beings is one of the final communications I had with them. One day in summer 2012 the handlers removed the frequency fence around me briefly to let me see how I really am. They let me taste freedom. They had been experimenting with letting me off periodically. Needless to say these few-and-far-between experiences felt awesome. I already knew I was undergoing Ascension and whenever off the force-field I felt incredible, extra-dimensional. The handlers, of course, read and captured this. They route it to my clone or other form of storage.

So I was in my house after work one day, with the force field removed and feeling about ten feet tall, bigger than my physical body's frame, totally supernatural. I was standing by my kitchen window and I got a very powerful and distressing message from Light Beings, as follows: **We're concerned you are collaborating with this military group. They are deceiving you. They will destroy you in a horrible way. Do not collaborate.**

My sense is they meant that the military will strip my psychic Ascension properties, and worse.

I went to lie down on my bed and I experienced another very disturbing energy flash. There was visual light—gold-white flashing light like what accompanied the previous communication minutes before. It was highly disturbing, communicating a kind of twistedness and back-stabbing associated with the black ops group—of what they were doing to me and would further do to me. It was expressed with a feeling of panic and urgency.

I know for a fact that my Light Beings are associated with Ascension, with the powerful multidimensional Megaverse Ascension communications I've experienced.

My heart breaks and cries all the time. I had incredible other-worldly heavenly Highs, fantastical contact and extra-dimensional experiences. Now they've been stolen from me by the most evil pieces of shit—pure evil, and used with my clone(s) to serve rats, used by "doctors" and "scientists." I'm left as a depleted, plastic tool.

Why am I not about "love and light"? I know, maybe if I just focus on love, listen to meditation music and raise my vibratory rate . . . !

Why haven't the Light Beings rescued me somehow? Why don't they rescue and protect other Starseeds this is happening to? Why don't they stop the military completely? They help us early on to some extent. I can piece that much together. Maybe behind the scenes they do some things, jump in at the most critical time. I really hate to say it. They know their energy signatures and communications are being electro-magnetically mapped by the military when they show up for someone who is already targeted. My house is a laboratory. Really. Invisible nano-tech devices communicating through a technology stack of ELF waves, HAARP, and other powerful transport technologies are all over my house. I'm not at liberty to say more.

Following are the only other insights I can come up with to this heartbreaking picture. We know through credible testimony by ex-Air Force personnel that Extra-terrestrial craft disabled nuclear equipment at highly secure facilities for decades. But do they show up and make public appearances all the time? Did they step in to stop the slaughter of millions of Iraqi civilians over the past few decades?

I no longer can pray as my spiritual essence is completely cut off from me. And even if I did, the evil military mad-scientists would capture any kind of ineffable response (which used to happen quite a bit). I'd rather be a spiritually dead mannequin than help these monsters. Think about that. Place yourself in my shoes and consider how horrible my situation is. I have something rare and precious and for that I'm trapped in a kind of real-life version of the movies *Angel Heart* and *The Matrix* (only the good guys don't win).

Light Being contact does not involve abductions but rather intimate contact of an angelic nature. I have experienced contact with other types of benevolent ET's by way of abduction. Some of these have been while asleep and some have been while awake. I am pressured to not discuss these in depth. I will only say that those who don't believe in ET's are ignorant. I do have to mention again that from March 2010 through most of 2011 that some of the experiences (while asleep) could have been induced by the "Branch A" black ops group. None of the highly positive ones were though and further I do tend to doubt that any of them aside from the obvious ones were. A couple of these contacts involved spacecraft.

One message I got from a visitor one morning was quite foreboding for mankind. After an astral, dream-like form of intercourse where I was semi-conscious she told me humans don't exist in the future, hinting the reason, perhaps, for her visit.

There was heavy alien visitation on this planet between 2009 and 2012.

- Interesting . . . as I'm typing this right now in an office after-hours, a woman in another row or cubicles is talking on the phone to a friend. They're talking about God. I kid you not. She's saying that it's not about going to church but having a personal relationship with God. "If you have a personal relationship with God, nothing can take that away from you," she says.

  Oh really?

Hopefully many readers will believe I am an acid casualty and chalk it all off to that. To those who have experienced, or ever do experience, LB's—keep your mouth shut unless you want to become a lab rat for the deep dark branches of the military. Only chat to trusted friends about it, and in person outdoors not over the phone. Never post anything about it online. You'll get picked up easily.

I've done everything I know to do to escape the military occupation. Everything, including humiliating acts to turn them off. It doesn't work. I have something they want badly. I've caused significant psychological, morale and organizational damage to them. I've fought back as best I can, learning, adapting and all the while trying to survive in the rat race and hold what's left of my family together.

CHAPTER 8

Ascension and the End of the Human Era
Part 1

"There's a war in Heaven. The Higher Intelligences, whoever they are, aren't all playing on the same team. Some of them are trying to encourage our evolution to higher levels, and some of them want to keep us stuck just where we are."—Grady McMurtry.

I'll say it again. Mankind is dead.

I could almost sum up this chapter by pointing you to a brief exchange between Dr. Robert Duncan and Jesse Ventura near the end of the excellent video documentary *Brain Invaders*. Duncan is Harvard-educated and worked for the CIA on the technology programs that facilitate electronic mind control. He tells Ventura frankly that yes these technologies exist and he was involved in their development but did not know what they would be used for. I believe him. Even if he did have any idea, I doubt he could have imagined they'd be turned on the American people. Further, he corrects Ventura, telling him that they are not being used to merely harass dissidents but to **torture** them. Ventura asks him if anything can be done to stop this (implying total control of all Americans). Duncan replies no, it's too late.

I'll augment the above. If one can see America as a hoodwinked puppet colony-nation within a portfolio of puppet colonies then it's clear that we're talking about global enslavement of the human species, not just Americans. I'd highly recommend Duncan's book *Project: Soul Catcher*.

The planet is enclosed in a frequency band, effectively an electro-magnetic wireless computer network where the computers are each and every human brain. The network topology basically consists of frequency waves from HAARP, GWEN towers (ELF waves), High Definition Digital TV and other sources, along with nanoparticles from chemtrails. Every brain and body are fully controllable down to the cellular level. A human (like me already) can be remotely, electronically controlled.

➢ What is Silent Sound Spread Spectrum (SSSS)?
➢ Why is High Definition Digital TV mandated by law now? It will be wired into the home of virtually every TV-watching slave in America. Why?
➢ Why are drones set to be deployed extensively over America?

The brain is a bio-computer. There were experiments going back many decades to interface it via microelectronic circuitry (computers). One of the pioneers in this evil was Jose Delgado. There is a great deal of disclosed documentation on his and others' experiments available online. Again, it can't be said in simpler terms: every human brain (and the body attached to it) is wide open to real-time remote control, electronically by computers, either by human operators of the computer or in an automated mode. Today, no implant is necessary. You may have heard about "the chip." You know, the one that will serve as the "mark of the beast"—some people call it an RFID and it's the size of a grain of rice. It's not needed now.

Not only can your thoughts, feelings, belief systems and sexuality be manipulated but your spiritual essence, soul and other psychic properties can be captured. Also, you can be put in a force field and thus be totally cut off from spiritual connections to Higher powers. This is what they've done to me. Rarely do the controllers (gangstalkers) disable the force field and allow me to actually feel/be myself, thus rarely to I have spiritual experiences.

In 2008 I started having beautiful lucid cosmic dreams. These were very deep, rich experiences with Heavenly settings, actually a blend of Heaven and Earth—Heaven on Earth. I now "live" in a Hell on Earth. I'm within a remote-controlled force field (frequency fence) and neurologically controlled by a team of "controllers" (gangstalking terrorists really).

As I write this it's a Sunday morning in February 2013 about 6 a.m. and there's a full moon in a cloudless sky. My head is ringing and faded voices of controllers are talking to me telling me to shut up. I wish I was free. Instead I'm as real as piece of plastic. I look back on my life and as I do some dude(s) at a military base monitor my reflections. I cannot engage in reverie without risk of put downs and other nasty interjections. As I said, I cannot even have regular dreams. All of my faculties are under total observation and control every single second, by the most powerful military force on the planet. Fact.

Saturday night used to be a holy night for me. I had various rituals I'd do. It was a time for reflection, introspection and memorializing losses; in general connecting to my God source. This day was especially potent to me on full moons. The human controllers in the evil black ops group know this of course. They hijack this, using me (my spirit) in their own rituals on this night. This is how despicable they truly are.

February 24, 2013 . . . I know they 'took me' sometime after midnight—I woke up around 4 a.m. While I can't be sure exactly what they did, I do know some of it involved communicating with another psychic I'm aware of. It's a redundant point, but this is, of course, against my will. This group is afraid of certain cosmic entities (from Sirius) and is wildly superstitious given their extremely narrow, dogmatic religious doctrine. They believe I have an association with some of these "hostile" entities and that there's a connection, based on my history, with Saturdays. Thus every Saturday night they mess with me to a) prevent any communication with the Sirius-associated entities as well as Light Beings; b) to hijack and use whatever extra-spiritual powers I may have and c) to study me more.

I don't like to share details on personal spiritual experiences but I'll tell you I had an amazing miracle that started on a Saturday night with a full moon some years ago. The synchronicities I had this night were off the scale. At one point I was driving and listening to a radio talk show. The speaker said the phrase "deer in the headlights" and a split second later, if that, a deer jumped out into the road staring straight into my headlights.

The magic I was experiencing in 2008 was Ascension related. It was Ascension energy.

The SEALs black ops group studied every pattern associated with and between myself and Light Beings and other entities. They either make sure I am asleep or they engage in some level of neurological interference, often torture, if they think I will be in contact with them. They also can induce a narcoleptic slumber any time they think I might be starting to have a multidimensional experience.

In the brief moments the controllers remove the force field and neurological control of my brain it sometimes poignantly hits me point blank: I have nothing in common with the humans around me. I am not one of them. They're sad, lost drones. It's not even that I don't want to have anything to do with them; I can't. There's no connection. To say they aren't sentient is a gross understatement. Putting it bluntly, they've been Archon-ized.

What do I mean by Archon-ized? As an example, last spring (2012) I was eating lunch at a crowded restaurant and started to have a multidimensional view. These experiences are totally involuntary and sudden. I must effectively be in a different dimension because the people and reality I see around me is like watching something on a movie screen. Nearly everyone around me appears to be a stunted, cartoon-like creature. I could hear the relay voice come on, communicating back to the controllers about it, and they started to capture it. The setting of people around me turned into a cartoon. It took on an almost two dimensional aspect. It was like watching a cartoonish sketch across time and space of another world, of an alien people. These were cattle I was watching, extremely dumb creatures bereft of purpose and of little essence at all. They were, in my reality, as fictional as a crude sketch. I have to say, quality paintings of humans in the past e.g. *The Mona Lisa* bear more resemblance to life than what I saw and see around me in these views.

These views of humanity as dead as cardboard continued throughout 2012 and increased in intensity closer to the end of the year. Given the extreme tortures I endured by the black ops group and the added insult of ignorant relatives et al. laughing at me with allusions to mental illness, I relished misanthropically the denouement of this game. After Thanksgiving, I experienced more of these views with stark profundity accompanied by a sort of confirmation of something quite welcome . . . I was ascended. It was clear I not just was split off from humankind but—I don't know if 'victorious' is the right word—given the context of being persecuted by the herd and its Archonic overlords, I was like a great Lion compared to a flea. I was totally separate. I still am no matter how soul-raped I am by my captors.

It must be considered that normal people may not have descended or changed at all. Perhaps it could be that it just appears that way from an ascended perspective.

As I type this and am monitored by the controllers, it presents an awkward feeling. I'm telling the truth and they don't like it. Imagine what it's like living with your perpetrators. Maybe it's not the full reason or full story, but there's little doubt to the significance that the rape of the human mind and soul by these groups is what put the nail in the coffin of mankind. Two respected researchers I spoke with recently as well as numerous other well educated people have said the same thing.

How bad is mind control under this group? How bad can it get? Here's an example. They don't want me to have these "views" of people as soul-less pieces of cardboard. This is a lot of the reason for stripping me of almost all of my psycho-spiritual properties. They don't want me to even remember my lower-dimensional views of people as cartoon characters. They give me a verbal and physical warning if a memory just pops into my mind, let alone if I try to recall one of the images. The warning usually consists of minor pain and is followed by more warnings and pain.

How's that for evil? I always make a mental statement to them reminding them that they killed mankind, not me. They say two things about it. 1) Yes, we know we did, we made a mistake. 2) You know that what you focus on expands; we can't let you think about it.

As another example, the handlers put me in a heavy drowsy state with aching head and toothache pains for reading text on the Mayan calendar while writing this book, citing the same "concerns."

This is reminiscent of the many months last year where they would CONSTANTLY tell me "stop thinking about that." This is how evil it gets. Can you imagine this?

Can you really?

And ironically . . . all this is why I'm still kept physically alive, why I'm still studied and used by my abductors/invaders. They vividly experience these multidimensional views via me, unfortunately the same way I do. It's just that now they use my clone and/or some kind of avatar or whatever technology in their lab. They intercept every type of energy coming and going from me and route these extrasensory experiences to their lab then feed it back to me. Impossible? They also still abduct me (per-se) and use me at "their place." Again, I'm about one hundred percent certain this is at a medical facility.

If any sensory experience, say a special nostalgic memory, even if it's simply recalling an aroma or an old song or a fleeting memory of an old grade school friend slips through the vectored filtering of my energy field, often the "spotter" will say "I'm on that, I'm there." This means they're checking it out, capturing it. They'll analyze the frequency signature and do a lookup in my mind.

There probably are two ways they can look through a mind to query a match and information for a given input. The mind can be seen as a filing cabinet as far as memories and storage of other information. If they've already cloned your brain to a computer they can look it up there. However, for a MILAB with super-soldier components, I believe the lookup can be done "in-place" in the target's mind, and in the background at that.

In the end, there are really only three parties who know what I'm writing here about my involuntary CRYSTAL CLEAR visions of humans as descended (or in a quarantine stasis) to be true: Myself, the black ops handlers and a tiny number of Starseeds of the same cloth as myself who have been left in this hell world as well.

February 24, 2013. It's 10 a.m. now. I went back to sleep a couple hours ago and paid the price for what I wrote so far in this chapter. I was tortured more with threats added. The ordeal concluded with a nasty image of my dead grandfather being sodomized. By the way, he was a decorated WWII veteran who fought on Normandy Beach. Proud to be an American, huh?

CHAPTER 9

Ascension and the End of the Human Era
Part 2

No matter what my captors do to me, in a sense it doesn't matter. Though I feel like I've been abandoned by my Light Beings, it doesn't matter. I know something happened. There was a dimensional shift. I exist beyond this hell and my soul is untouchable. This forsaken hell world is just that. It was a fallen world to begin with, wasn't it? It's gone. The dark side totally rules this planet now and the level of suffering that the recessed human population will go through now will be unlike anything in the past. I was talking briefly on a radio show last night about the topic of the dark-side NWO stealing souls—de-souling mankind. I was not on long. I just gave a brief narrative of what the military is doing. The main guest was asked what he thought of this. He said it's the end of mankind, again. This kind of tampering with Celestial design has resulted in previous extinctions of versions of man on this planet, he said. I can't speak to that though I've heard this theory before and it's more than plausible. But I KNOW based on my Ascension-related multiversal experiences that this version of mankind has already bit the dust. You can thank the monsters who have spiritually raped Starseeds in the name of "science" instead of protecting them.

If I go far back into childhood I can recall experiences that could be described as Ascension-related. It's silly to think in a linear fashion though. As a mind-control torture victim this is especially painful since one thought leads to the next and the 'wrong' thought/memory can get you punished or provide something sacred and valuable to be desecrated by your torturers. A better way of looking at your life is something I learned from Taoist philosophy. See your life as one big event—I visualize it geometrically as a sphere, not a linear timeline. From that context, whatever I'm going through *at the moment* is cast against the backdrop of my entire life. There is no past or future. It's one big experience. This has a diminishing effect on the circumstances of the present.

I had some amazing supernatural experiences, as I've said, in the mid and late 2000's. I also had terrible events in my personal life. I know what it's like to get a phone call at night with surprising, devastating news about a family member. I know what it's like to have multiple Category 5 shit-storms going on at once. All the major stuff. Retreating from the human jungle—from the matrix and its barbed wire games—was essential. The three things I had, and unfortunately I stress 'had', were: my mind, love and God. Under the God category I definitely include Light Beings and other kick-ass benevolent ET's; and, of course, boundless ineffable spirituality. In my inner world, my inner personal life, with these blessings I had something that was seemingly untouchable, beautiful beyond comparison. This is what the SEALs black ops group has stolen from me. All of it. This is why I say I'm dead.

Back in 2007 while unwinding up in the mountains it hit me like a ton of bricks one day. Something wants me dead and something wants me alive. For every sick thing that's been foisted on me the proverbial cavalry has come to the rescue at the last minute. I got the impression that there was more to this than a haphazard coincidental pattern. It really struck me that there might be a spiritual war of some kind. I deeply dislike what I see as the Archonic (Abrahamic) 'god'. This is the bastard ET who essentially rules the planet, the devil. Too, I've always felt a strong kind of "pull" or affinity with the ancient world. I somehow resonate with soldiers in the Roman era. What that, of course, means is a spiritual lineage. I think it's safe to say I'm an old soul.

Becoming solipsist: You can't have a healthy relationship with a sick person(s). By extension of this, as the father of existentialism, Sartre, put it . . . "Hell is other people."

If you surround yourself with enough people and let them poison your spirit then this definition is fully correct. We, in what *was* Western Civilization, exist in an anti-world. It is comprised of falsifications and hoaxes layered and interwoven in myriad permutations. The average mind is nothing but a supernumerary participant, a figment of this manipulated dream. But an important supernumerary it is. In fact, mediocrity is the highest valued quality in society today, thus the most highly praised trait and behavior. When I was a kid in the 1970's there was a saying, "do your own thing." This maxim is spat upon today. Greatness does not smack of duplicity but rather oddity.

It's important to realize just how sick the sheeple are. Those truly sentient and free in mind do not subscribe to consensual reality. But living in a mental police state you must fake it, you must blend in. I hope, by witness of my ordeal and the reality of physical electronic mind control you can understand why. By the way, the definition of the word Occult is simply "hidden." What does one hide, truth or lies? You hide the truth—that which is valuable or otherwise sensitive must be protected and hidden, and conversely you promote lies. There's an old adage: Lies are shouted and the truth is whispered behind closed doors.

With the dissolution of traditional family structures and total fragmentation of society many people who retain their intellects are becoming solipsist. This trend of anomie was actually described decades ago in the book *Future Shock*. Many reasonably intelligent people have to be in a state of bewilderment when they look at the world around them, when they look at what America is today. Most however are just idiots who live to consume and follow fashion trends.

It's a funny thing, an awkward thing to face, and decision to make . . . that is, breaking away from society. The right term is divorce. I made this choice (or maybe it was made for me) long ago on some deep-down level, but I emphatically reaffirmed it in the mid-2000's. I proclaimed to myself that mainstream society is sick and ignorant and I want no part of it. I meant and mean it. Being solipsist was and is a big part of my constitution. I can't stress enough that being duplicitous and Fabian must also be employed to survive with minimal damage.

I turned heavily to metaphysics as I slammed the door on consensual reality (a.k.a bullshit). In standard modern psychology this is called "magical thinking," meaning mental illness. I'm laughing.

> ➢ How many Americans support(ed) the "War on Terror?" How many believe the magical story about the killing of Osama Bin Laden (the man, the myth the legend!)? How many Americans are on psychiatric medicine? I haven't done a survey myself but I've heard it's something like one in four.

I postulate that numerous tribes of ET's have jumped into happenings on this planet (more obtrusively than cosmic law allows) over the past five or so years. Based on some lucid dreams I had as well as direct communications with "my guys" there is absolutely no doubt that there was a spiritual war, or maybe I should say battles (within a more protracted war) on this planet in this time frame. I believe it was reconciled at least partially but, of course, I just speculate.

I believe that powerful forces of good and evil were at full-blown war between 2009 and 2012.

I know there are only an infinitesimal number of people on this planet who are like me. I know them when I see them or hear their description of certain phenomena. While we are ascended out of this dump, we are physically still trapped here. I cannot stress strenuously enough, again, this place called Earth is the gutter (from here on out).

I could cry my eyes out, waiting, begging for and wondering when the Light Beings, when one of "my guys" is going to do something about my enslavement and free me. And honestly I feel some anger, wondering why in the hell they let this happen, why they haven't freed me. Is there a higher purpose to me being enslaved and tortured? Doubtful.

The bottom line is that some funny things, odd Ascension type energies, may still be going on but I believe, short of a real surprise, it's all over. Everything worthwhile has been evacuated from Earth and what's left is a non-spiritual, non-cosmic plantation for the Archons. How it's different now than from say twenty years ago is that it will now go into full physical enslavement of the masses, full-blown Transhumansim.

CHAPTER 10

Lucy, Transhumansim and the 2012 Galactic Alignment

The term *Luciferianism* seems to be tossed about more often in discussions regarding our world today. What is it, who is Lucifer? It's far more myth and lore than anything else. This is another topic unto itself but let's take it for a spin.

There's of course the Christian definition of Lucifer. Naturally this is total mishmash gibberish ignorance, not even cohesive enough to be called good dogma. Lucifer here distills to "the devil" which ironically is Jehovah himself. In fact, in a way, Lucy bears the same enigmatic qualities as Judeo-Christianity, just without the painful brain-twisting mental illness baked into it.

There are two types of Christians I know of. The people who go to a church, engage in macabre rituals, drink the Kool-Aid and give their souls/psychic energy away to dark forces; and those who do not but rather follow the principles taught by Jesus. This book is not intended to create controversy or antagonize those who follow Semitic religions, but an honest look at the troubled history of x, y or z and its offshoots is a scary look to be sure. It's a look that paints the picture of our insane world quite well.

61

Lucifer is mentioned only one time in the bible, referenced as Venus the morning star and is not linked to anything evil. This reference could also be a historical reference to Babylonian king Nebuchadnezzar. *Dante's Inferno*, to my knowledge, is where the definition and promotion of Lucifer as an evil character originated entirely. This book is of course fiction.

It's interesting that the Mayan calendar started with the birth of the planet Venus on August 12, 3114 BC. Ancient Mayan astronomers noted that the previous age started with the creation of Venus and ended on the winter solstice 2012 with the Galactic alignment involving Venus.

One view of Lucy is as a positive entity, a true friend to mankind. Is Lucifer the Light Bearer who helped man out of the dark when he was a grunting cave-dweller (and has ever since), giving him a spark of intelligence and careening a wind beneath his sail? Is he that unsung hero? Could he, or she if you like, be the fire-fighter accused of being the arsonist? Even entertaining this thought, the biblical warning about the Great Deceiver always comes to mind. The Great Deceiver though would apply to any kind of enlightenment though right? It's always "Satan/Lucifer" behind the scenes promoting tricks—things that look good on the surface but ensnare us.

Luciferianism in the context of a movement or philosophy that has the best interest of mankind is certainly a good thing. This means the creation of a new man and it is not a new concept. Nietzsche talked almost prophetically about the Overman, and certainly the concept of a new and better man well predates Nietzsche's era; for that matter we have to consider the influence of the ancient world on Nietzsche. The point is that this idea has been around a long time.

So there seems to be a modified socio-political definition of Luciferianism associated with Transhumansim: the planning or putting into operation the creation of a new man. This means a New World Order. There are inherent winners and losers in this to say nothing of explicit ones unless we're to believe egalitarianism isn't a charade and kind of temporary wrecking-ball used by the global elite. A clear master-slave model based on racial and socio-political lines is used in Transhumansim just as it was in the ancient world; this model is what will unabashedly be reinstituted.

What are other definitions of Luciferianism or Lucifer? Carte blanche. You provide the definition and motif! I must say that I've experienced wicked lower astral characters—and my psychic senses linked them with the powerful global elite on the planet and ironically these people call themselves (as I understand) Luciferians. However, by no means do certain global elite nor does anyone have a license on Lucifer. Further, from my research Lucifer is dualistic, both Celestial and human, and marked by good and bad. I personally see both sides.

In the transhumanist world the Celestial aspect of man is being ripped out and replaced with totally man-made components. That's a fact. Where science and God may have been interconnected they now are opposites. I totally disagree that Lucifer—or any Higher Intelligence with any respect or liking for mankind would ever be party to this.

Let me point out something about the archons, the global elite.

1. They obviously, undoubtedly, have had a great deal of help, a kind of "invisible hand" from an evil ET/deity. That would be Jehovah.

2. They can call themselves Luciferians, Christians, x, y or z but they thrive on enigmatic motifs or mention-at-your-own-risk exclusive race cults. They will bastardize anything that is public and rework their own version of it thus stealing it in a way. If you control the media, furthermore, you can totally falsify and rewrite anything by creating new memes for the masses.

One can see how Luciferianism provides a backdrop and larger historical context to Transhumansim with attachments to the "one true god," described in various secret societies, none-other than "the man"! But I think we have a case of mistaken identity. Lucifer is not the devil. Trust me, I know the devil and it is not Lucifer. The problem is that the meme (mind virus) of Lucifer being one and the same as the devil is so strong.

Praying to Lucifer to deliver man from evil and tragedy would have been a great thing. If the Light Bearer was cast out by Jehovah/Yahweh and we live in an age of darkness (Christians say we do live in a fallen world) then what does this tell us about this "god" Jehovah/Yahweh?

"Lucifer" just gets too abstract from here though. "Lucifer" may be better treated as a body of principles than as a deity.

For what it's worth, the word Satan is not a title. It's a Hebrew word meaning enemy or adversary.

➢ Are there any Higher Intelligences that are enemies of the devil?

There has been an ongoing battle in very recent history between the devil and Ascension. Mankind has a pimp: the devil—whom he has been tricked into calling God. This pimp first presented himself to the demented old desert pervert Abraham. The devil promises man that things will improve albeit via a difficult struggle, and at some stage man can ascend, having greater control and power over the world. But which men does he promise this to?

This imposter god does not really have access to the human soul or he didn't, at least not easy access. He must always find a way to hijack it. He has successfully used man himself to do this via the military industrial complex. To my knowledge he's having amazing success and as I say I believe it's a done deal. If I've done my job correctly, relating this is what this book is mostly about.

As I see it—and I can neither logically or intuitively see it any other way—a war between the lower astral realm and the Galactic Center is either still going on or will heat up again. The lower astral and its "god" rule over this hell planet. The human soul is a powerful thing. Since it is now captured (those of the masses and to whatever extent those of Starseeds as well) and thus available to the devil (Jehovah) it may well be used against Celestial entities, God if you like.

By deduction you could call this a war between what was man (let's call him now robo-man) and Heaven.

Man could have been saved and ascended into a higher dimensional being. Instead he was ripped off. His soul was/is being stolen and he exists in an ever more synthetic, false "reality." A robot in every respect. Man unwittingly sold his soul for smoke and mirror gimmicks. The deal the Indians got for Manhattan Island was great compared to what mankind got for the bliss of ignorance and distraction.

Back to the Mayans

The following from *The Mayan Prophecies* (Adrian G. Gilbert and Maurice Cotterell) is a perfect metaphor for what was supposed to and could have been man's ascension at the cusp of the new age, in the year 2012.

"In the spiritual traditions of the West the serpent (or sometimes dragon), as well as symbolizing the path of the sun through the sky, represents the lower self. According to Gnostic traditions, each one of us is born as a serpent and constrained to a life of crawling in the dust of the earth. Just as a serpent renews itself by casting off its skin and growing a new one, so we ourselves live life after life dying and being reborn, but still unable to raise ourselves from the earth. In this state of unawareness we are cut off from the higher worlds of spirit and remain the helpless brood of the great Solar Serpent. Thus it is that as the fallen children of Adam and Eve we are imprisoned in our renewable 'skins' and constrained to live life after life and to experience death after death in the material world. This is why Coatlicue, like her Hindu equivalent Kali, has a necklace of skulls and dismembered hands, for the earth mother takes as well as gives life. However, Gnostic traditions also speak of a cosmic destiny, of the possibility inherent in humans as souls of leaving the physical earth to journey to our true home on higher, non-material planes. This is the essence of the spiritual teachings of all the great masters including Jesus, Buddha, Muhammad and, we can presume the original Quetzalcoatl-Kukulcan.

Yet all of them teach, if we read their words carefully, that to gain freedom requires a transformation of our being. To use another metaphor, the ordinary human lives as a caterpillar on the cabbage-leaf of life. Here he or she can live a thousand times without even being aware of the possibility of further development. Yet, just as the caterpillar has within it the potential to be transformed into a beautiful butterfly, so too the human has the possibility of metamorphosing into a higher form. We do not have to remain at the caterpillar stage of life forever: we too can become angels—even while alive in the physical body."

*   *   *

The train came by but only some got on board.

CHAPTER 11

Beyond Evil

Before reading this passage you must understand the power and capabilities of neurological programming. It is maddening to listen to people who are knowledgeable about such topics as chemtrails, nanotech, mind control, implants, super soldiers/ MILABs etc. who don't comprehend the fact that if a remote party can control your brain then they can make you do almost anything and THERE IS NOTHING YOU CAN DO ABOUT IT. Willpower is great. I have strong willpower. But willpower will not defeat electronic mind-brain control. For one thing, the alter personality programming, hellish synthetic nightmares and myriad other programming done to you when you are asleep is indefensible. The target is totally defenseless, totally helpless. The mind has no firewall.

When handlers (gangstalkers) are talking to you (voices in your head) via synthetic telepathy you cannot "override" it, you can't drown it out etc. I tried so many homemade cognitive therapy types of tricks to defeat this, to deal with it, to mess with it, it's not even funny. I must have two or three notebooks full of mental tactics I've come up with. I tried different types of meditations. Meditation fails miserably. Listen to me, under a synthetic existence the self is gone! To the extent it lingers at all, it's a continually wounded dying thing. Any thought you have, ANY—is pointless. Your whole mental and even emotional function can be fully controlled. The handlers can put any image they want in your mind. Imagine images of your children, of dead relatives, grandparents etc., being sodomized. Your own mind and memories are used against you to provide the characters and settings. Yep, they've done this, and worse created movies of this in my mind. They've replayed some of the most cherished settings from my childhood; they started off blissfully and then they stopped it and as I woke up they told me they would go through every precious memory I've ever had and pervert it if I didn't do x, y or z.

Mostly these threats are to coerce me to stop having certain thoughts! How do you do that? How do you have a foreign voice/thought transmitted into your head telling you for hours not to think of something . . . and then *not* think of it?

Can you imagine—evil idiots torturing you day and night and you obviously develop vicious negative thoughts about them and various pathologies. The way their equipment is set up they have to experience your thoughts and emotions the same way (although they can turn down the intensity somewhat to protect themselves). It pisses them off when you think of something gross or really negative, and to retaliate against your natural repelling-type reactions they torture you more! That's exactly what they did (and still do) to me.

These monsters tortured me with horrific nightmares that are almost too painful to describe simply for having thoughts they didn't like. Remember this when you hear the term mind control. To my knowledge no other MILAB has ever been tortured like this. And they did/do it almost every single night—well past the "break-in period." They did things to me that you wouldn't do to POW's.

How am I still alive? How am I not in a mental hospital? Behold the miracle of neurological programming and a wonder drug that can revitalize you and keep you going even after a near-sleepless night. Conditions like PTSD can be fixed, at least temporarily, by reprogramming your brain. It's truly amazing. After a year of torture they started to apply these astonishing fixes. They have given me a terrifying lucid nightmare and/or twisted "mental mutilation" with eerie sounds of family members calling out to me and distant echoing voices and bizarre time-space feelings . . . and . . . kept me in a good mood as I awakened out of it (to mitigate psychological/emotional damage). They can take an event like a funeral where you should be wrenched with sorrow and make you feel happy instead.

They can do this to anybody, anytime. Are you figuring it out? I can call somebody for support and they can make what I tell that person go in one ear and out the other. They can make someone easily think you are mentally ill, bad, lying, joking, etc . . . whatever—sky's the limit! What don't you understand about FULL CONTROL of any human brain, anytime, instantly, for any purpose?

For the last time, the human brain is a computer with no firewall and we live in an open, public wi-fi world. You're all defenseless and you're all fucked.

- Note, to the intelligence community. In stating the above, I'm not disclosing any classified information that isn't already published on the Internet. Further, as we know, the odds of anyone who is not on the inside believing this are infinitesimal, and it's far too late for anything to be done about it.

In some of the worst instances of torture the handler told me afterwards "Remember, I can do this to you every night for the rest of your life and there's nothing you can do about it."

And he's right, he absolutely can.

Around my birthday in 2012, the torturers personally hated me so much they did try to kill me. Because they've reportedly spent over $100 million on me it's difficult to do. There's red tape and they have to really be able to justify it; it has to come down as an order from high command. However, *accidents* can happen. The target can be driven to suicide or a mental hospital (where they'll likely never see the light of day). They prevented me from having bowel movements. To even have a small bowel movement, I had to pledge that I was one of them and loyal to them while on the toilet. This went on for two to three weeks. During this time, they also kept me up all night on several occasions. When I would start to fall asleep they'd pulse me—running a shivering, unpleasant kind of shock through my body which would jolt me awake. I truly believed this was the end. My mental state was being totally broken. This was hardcore torture. I needed to sleep so bad but wasn't allowed. Cruelly they'd let me start to go under, perhaps be asleep for a minute then jolt me awake. I went into a state of disbelief. I remember saying aloud, "my God, this is it, this is the end." I'd go out onto my back porch and light a candle and *try* to communicate with Light Beings.

Apparently around October 2012, some of the worst handlers or their "team lead" were thrown out. This is because I got braver and started reaching out, going public. One of the goals in MK-Ultra is to terrorize you and keep you isolated, feeling helpless. I'll forever be grateful to Solaris Blue Raven's book *Programmed by Deception* for providing the catalyst for this. This book resonated with me tremendously, although the entities involved in her story are in the entertainment industry. It motivated me to create my website starseedresistance.com. This site started one night in September 2012 sometime around 3 a.m. following a torture. I simply started blogging my experiences. It was difficult because I was being, of course, monitored and threatened, interfered with. And I was dead tired. Why did they allow me to do this in the first place though? Good cop/bad cop. It is part of the brand of MK-Ultra psychology they use.

- If you are a Starseed, if you have paranormal abilities, are into metaphysics etc., do not go to starseedresistance.com. You will get picked up by the military and thoroughly checked out. You are getting all you need to know in this book.

Not only did I start publishing events to this website but I began calling Special Operations groups of different branches of the military, often in the early morning hours following torture. I'd tell them exactly who I was, where I was calling from, and that I was a torture victim in an insane mad-science project of a black ops group of the SEALs. Occasionally I actually got an intelligence officer on the phone. Surprisingly, they often heard me out and made some recommendations. Still they were tight-lipped, for good reason. What are they supposed to say? The point is, knowing that my phone and Internet use are under surveillance by various intelligence agencies, I took advantage of this to yell out that my life was in danger and let them know the atrocities being committed. It did help. Often the tortures lightened up or would stop, for the night. Once in a while, I'd get a positive synthetic dream instead of a nightmare. These were usually later around 6 a.m. This would be done by the handlers, I believe, to cover their tracks. Yes, they can create blissful, euphoric dreams as well.

In playing the good cop part of the good cop/bad cop game, some of my handlers have created images in my mind of a human (me) encased in a desktop computer, trying to pull the casing off of me and saying "I can't get this thing off me." They've let up at other times, as I've mentioned before, on the force field around me and let me feel my actual self, my natural self as I was and would be, without the synthetic robo-human properties and surrounding force field and stripped-out spiritual essence. They did this to dangle the prize of freedom in front of me. I can't remember how many times they told me I'd be free by such and such date.

Christmas 2012 was one of the dates I was supposed to be freed. Under mind control and relentless psychological tactics the depressed, sleep-deprived manipulated target is easily duped into believing these scams. There's a part of you that buys into it even though it fits the same pattern of lies you've heard a million times. This is because you crave your liberation so desperately; a part of you can't help but want to believe it. To underscore the point of how powerful neurological mind control is, they can make you sad and tearful at the thought of bidding them farewell! "We've been through a lot together. We go back a long way now," are some of the things they say to you during these faux farewells. You've heard the expression "they have me by the balls." How about "they have me by the limbic—?" To keep you from becoming too despondent, from dwelling on the fact that you are totally "owned" they keep the lure and promise of eventual freedom mixed in with the rest of their dialogs.

To give you an idea of the extent to which they suppress me, they inflict torture if I:

- Sleep with crystals or rocks by me
- Try to meditate
- Focus on the Sun / Sunlight
- Look at the clouds, sky or any landscape the "wrong way"
- Look at any humans the "wrong way"
- Remember the lower-dimensional real-cartoon-encapsulated views of humans I had in 2012. The last clear one I had, by the way, was in late January 2013. As I've said, they've effectively stripped and/or blocked my spiritual properties, putting them in my clone.

In other words, if I even try to pray or have any kind of spiritual connection they "come down on me" to use their term for torture. They create toothaches, headaches, intensify ringing in ears, put pressure on my head, create twitching in an eye or make my forehead suddenly wrinkle then unwrinkle, create a sensation in my kneecaps of being beaten with a pipe.

They've been quite honest at times, telling me there's only one way out. You can guess what. My response is Fuck You. Never. I have an obligation to try to live as long as I can, no matter what. On that topic, many nights I've been awakened to a handler telling me to kill myself, graphically telling me to put a gun in my mouth. Sometimes I've awoken without them knowing it, pretending to be still asleep, and heard them programming me to do this as well as other awful things.

I refuse to participate in evil. I'm thrilled that I'm a failed project. I'm not thrilled that I'm a POW, right here in America, in a nightmare that few could believe. I'm a U.S. citizen and a massive torture victim and POW yet I can't prove it. I'm not alone though. I assure you that the hordes of prisoner-torture victims in archon prisons like Guantanamo all around the world can believe it. Thousands of other American dissidents who are Targeted Individuals can believe it.

It is March 18, 2013 1:22 a.m. I don't use military time anymore. I always write the time as am/pm. It's a stupid little thing but it helps me disassociate myself with my perpetrators. They woke me up a little while ago and started talking to me and torturing me. As they admit, it's another night of sleep deprivation. It makes the accidental "heart attack" look more natural. In contrast, they at least used to let me (actually forced me) to exercise. Again, it's now been 15 months since this began with the SEALs. The only point in still doing this is to drive me to suicide or a total mental breakdown which would result in the same thing just on a slower, crueler scale. Now they're torturing my dog who's sitting next to me, for writing this paragraph, making him convulse. There's so much more I could have said in this book but didn't out of greater concerns. Yes, there are things worse than me being murdered.

By the way, one of the things they threatened me with early on if I didn't cooperate was to send me to Guantanamo. Also, lately they've threatened to keep me in a coma in the lab at the (unnamed) international medical research facility where they have my clone, near Emory University, indefinitely so they can get as much use out of me as possible, then kill me in a controlled death environment and monitor my soul.

One thing that brings me immense satisfaction is knowing that clones of these black ops personnel will be used in the future (if they aren't already). This is due to the super secrecy of their operations and technology. It's much smarter to use clones of existing personnel than to rely on many new recruits. Few people could probably handle being torturers and living with the insanity of these operations. Also, various forms of clones could be made to be more callous and possibly lack any empathy at all. In the major end-game these black ops personnel are nothing but liabilities and security concerns— big ones—especially given the excessive paranoia of the archons. The "real" guy who works as a handler will be put away and his clones (or another work-force) will be used. The promise of a great future in the New World Order will never be delivered to these people. It wasn't designed for them.

> ➢ What did Henry Kissinger have to say about "military men"?

The true New World Order and their ilk will live like kings and can certainly live forever via cryogenics and mind uploading. Do some research on these key words and see what you find. It's real and it's here today. The best way to learn about Transhumanism is from the proponents of it. Many of these people are brilliant. They like to call themselves things like "futurists" and they talk about Transhumanist technologies and paradigms like it's off in the future but it isn't in the future.

I promise solemnly, the more they torture me, the longer they keep me imprisoned, the more sick things they do with my soul/ spirit via my clone, the worse things will get for humanity . . . not by my actions though. As I've stated, the human race is already dead. They're just zombies right now. All I know is on some level, in some cosmic way there will be retribution for these crimes.

Although I'm a civilian I decided a while back to join Oath Keepers. What are Oath Keepers doing about the electronic torture and enslavement of American citizens? They vow to uphold the Constitution and refuse orders to harm the American people, yet listening to most of them they are obsessed and distracted with the "gun grab" threat which is more theatre than anything. The Powers That Be love it when the masses arm themselves with primitive caveman weapons. I've already explained, as have others, that the government can simply program everyone who they don't like who owns a gun to shoot their family and friends (fellow comrades) and themselves. Sandy Hook etc., is a small scale example (that's probably what happened). They can instantly make a group of armed civilians/ militia throw their weapons down, strip naked and dance around in the street singing nursery rhymes if they want. *(Note, this is pure speculation, totally unbelievable to 99% of the American public and does not constitute leaking of classified information).*

*   *   *

Welcome to the machine

I have some harsh news for the denizens of this planet, especially for those already suffering from electronic torture. The only thing that can end electronic torture and enslavement is for a global cataclysm like a major EMP (electro-magnetic pulse). The whole grid has to go down, lights out. That would be another nightmare and the odds of this happening anyway are rather slim. There's no shielding, nothing that can stop the carrier waves we are bathed in. Consider the very term "mind control." There is no political solution and no chance for *actual* revolution despite what the "alternative" media suggests.

Chapter 12

Conclusions

Man was an ignorant, superstitious, stunted creature, some races worse than others. Clearly Caucasians, a suicide cult, were the most afflicted. You see, man was easily programmed to subscribe to a catalog of memes. The very sight of a forbidden geometrical symbol, say a cross with the ends bent at right angles, or a pentagram could make our subject skip a heartbeat and be filled with negative emotions. Yes, the sight of a symbol was enough to incite violence. Man was self-programmed to function within a narrow band of ideas and mentation. This narrow, constricted band is called *normalcy*. Punishment, whether passive or extreme was delivered when openly deviating beyond what's normal, when getting "out of band."

Anyone with ideas/solutions or abilities to elevate Mankind, to pull him out of the ditch and straighten him out, was persecuted by the very herd he might have tried to help as soon as he opened his mouth and was found out about. And of course, his wares were, behind the scenes, stolen and applied by the authorities in a bastardized way to enhance their power; and the act of it covered up.

Well, I've told it like it is. I've told my story. In closing I must again express my hatred for the invaders, terrorists, thieves—the SEALs black ops group. They robbed me of my greatest riches and committed atrocities so sick and perverted I cannot fully talk about them, let alone publish them for the sake of my family. They call themselves champions of mankind, admit they made mistakes and say that they have to be brutal and cruel. No comment.

I have been a huge Nietzsche fan for many years. *Thus Spoke Zarathustra* was like a bible to me. Despite my extreme bitterness of being a MK-Ultra torture victim and mind and soul slave—and to boot being surrounded by self-imprisoning candycane-flag-waving morons who talk about "freedom," I will violate a core tenet of Nietzsche and express a bit of pity for erstwhile man. I don't hate him. I forgive him and feel for the great tragedy that has been his history.

But martyr myself, no way.

You my friend, if you are not of this world, keep your mouth shut! Disguise yourself, blend in. Choose a weakness for yourself to hide behind—say to the sheep that you are a drug addict, alcoholic, have depression, suffer from a rare physical ailment or suffer from cancer etc. Never display yourself as an individual *and* strong. The ideals of the forsaken Founding Fathers and their principles are a fairy tale and always were. Again my friend: *Thus Spoke Zarathustra* . . . the herd will do you worse than death, they will desecrate you. You can't have a healthy relationship with a sick person, nor sick persons. What is special and sacred about mankind lies solely in the Higher individual and is experienced thus, never en-masse. What is special about mankind is Nothing! It exists outside of him and few have connection to it, few even want it. May this tiny occulted flicker be somehow kept alive for the very few who have it during the unbelievable hell that lies ahead.

It's a great honor to be acknowledged by the world's most powerful, advanced military by way of being hunted, tortured, studied, weaponized and imprisoned, under watch by a team of a half dozen or more personnel every single second. I've been hunted in the Matrix since the day I barely emerged into it.

- I've used the term "Ascend" greatly in this book. Perhaps a better word is "Evacuate."

I've told you the Greatest Secret, about 2012 and Ascension/ Descension, though few may believe it. The cosmic Mayan snake and eagle have joined. The lower energies of man (snake—Kundalini) merged with the Celestial (eagle). Reincarnation has stopped. A very few people ascended during this window of time though. The rest are walking cardboard now. The world you see around you is illusion, a joke. It is a quarantined dimension.

Here is my favorite Nietzsche maxim. It's on his concept of self-overcoming:

> *"Life itself confided to me this secret . . . behold it said, I am that which must overcome itself again and again."*

This may no longer be valid.

The human race is damned. I always had one foot outside of this world. As I said at the beginning, humanity is like a bad car accident that I'm driving by. I'd rather not look. I don't want to be involved. For what humans, collectively, have done to me alone, they're damned in my book—in the sense that I'll NEVER help them. But it's a moot point anyway. You'll see.

Am I a Walter Mitty? You're dreaming. I went to great lengths to live quietly. I still got picked up. Publicity is the last thing I wanted. I wrote this book because I had to. Anyone who wants to be in a black ops group as a MILAB especially as a "super psychic" (lab rat) is a retard. I never asked for this. I begged and did unbelievable stuff to try to get out. I will get out one way or another. On the most important level I am free. I ascended and exist beyond this prison planet. I have to and do believe that.

Some readers may dismiss me as a lunatic but I assure you, two parties know the truth: I and my captors. In their own words they've told me "we know what we are and what we've done to you. We fucked up. We have to cover it up and live with it."

The Mayans were right

I know a truth that few on this planet know and I've published it in this book. Classified space-age technologies aren't a big deal anymore. I certainly don't care. Man's best stuff is nothing compared to real Ascension or real, benevolent ET's. If you understand that the human race is being put under direct electronic mind, body and soul control then you know it's over. For that reason alone—"seeing the writing on the wall"—it's over. What I personally have *seen* psychically as I've described it in this book is the end. This world is already totally synthetic, lampooned and quarantined in a squalid dead-zone dimension. It's a perversion, a mistake and it has been written off. It's been archived. The devil and his archons won (at least in part) no matter how things appear. The awesome Ascension energy, true multidimensional Ascension, was shut out. The SEALs continue to use me in this regard, in what they've stolen from me but it will never work for them. I **Will** that every energy, every supernatural property they have ever taken from me be cursed and backfire catastrophically on them at the worst possible time.

There are a number of people who have been involved in the science and operations of these projects and technologies (which have collectively killed mankind) who have been killed for posing a threat, for trying to come forward. God only knows how many people, normal and gifted alike, civilian and military, who have been tortured as lab rats to perfect the technologies used in the greatest crime in history.

To the military industrial complex: Nice Shot. You whacked mankind.

I wish I'd resisted and fought the invaders harder earlier on. They never let up and I was ignorant, totally blindsided.

What I had spiritually up until December 2011 was fantastic, beyond this world.

Despite my circumstances and disabled connection to the spiritual realm, I still long for and cling to my memories of Light Beings.

I don't know why I was really brought here to this hell planet and why I was left here imprisoned by the military. There could be many reasons. However, I believe that everyone who was spiritually evacuated *Won*—their physical body only remains here in the matrix as an animated mannequin puppet.

*   *   *

All my heart and love go to Light Beings and every other Higher Intelligence that's helped me in this twisted life in the Matrix. This book is dedicated to them.

The END.

Printed in the United States
By Bookmasters